Magic of Impromptu Speaking

Create a Speech That Will Be Remembered for Years in Under 30 Seconds

Andrii Sedniev

Magic of Impromptu Speaking

Create a Speech That Will Be Remembered for Years in Under 30 Seconds

Published by Andrii Sedniev

Copyright © 2013 by Andrii Sedniev

ISBN 978-1-62209-747-0

First printing, 2013

www.MagicOfPublicSpeaking.com

PRINTED IN THE UNITED STATES OF AMERICA

Dedications

This book and my love are dedicated to Olena, my wife and partner, who makes every day in life worthwhile. Thank you for supporting me on every stage of development of *Magic of Impromptu Speaking* system and giving encouragement when I needed it the most. Without you, this book might never have been finished.

I also want to dedicate this book to all past students of the *Magic of Impromptu Speaking* system who by their success inspire me to become a better person every day.

Contents

Why learn impromptu speaking?

Every day you speak with relatives, friends and strangers without needing preparation. Talking off the cuff, one on one is easy for most of us. When the quality of an impromptu speech is crucial, however, giving it becomes a huge problem.

How did you feel when you were asked to give an impromptu speech for the first time? I remember my grandma's birthday celebration 20 years ago, where my mom said, "Andrii, the next toast will be yours."

"Mom, please no! I don't know what to say."

"I am not going to discuss it with you, Andrii. You are next!"

I thought, "Oh, my god! The time passes so quickly! I will have to talk in just two minutes and I have no idea what to say! Everybody will see my embarrassment and I will feel so miserable."

Imagine that you are giving an interview live on CNN or answering a CEO's question in a boardroom. When the pressure is on for a high-quality speech, most speakers' minds go blank.

One answer during the job interview may determine whether you get the job of your dreams or not. One answer during the Q&A session may determine how potential customers perceive your competence. One answer during the TV debates may determine whether you become the president or not.

No matter what you do, you will encounter situations where you need to speak impromptu, and success in life may be determined by your impromptu speaking skills. Great

1

impromptu speakers are extremely successful during TV interviews, Q&A sessions, networking events and even prepared speeches. Audiences love speakers who can go off script and improvise on stage. Those who can speak well off the cuff are better communicators, are more creative and have more interesting and versatile lives.

The good news is that you can become an outstanding impromptu speaker very quickly if you follow the right process.

What is Magic of Impromptu Speaking?

During the last 10 years, I collected tips, techniques and strategies that can dramatically raise the level of any speaker in impromptu speaking. My goal was to create the most comprehensive system, which will make anyone a world-class impromptu speaker within a very short time. The *Magic of Impromptu Speaking* system was based on the analysis of thousands of impromptu speaking contests, interviews, debates and Q&A sessions.

The results were astonishing. *Magic of Impromptu Speaking* students reported that not only did their ability to speak off the cuff improve significantly over a period of 2 months, but their lives also changed for the better.

Those who speak well impromptu, on average, get promotions faster, are more interesting to be around and are more creative in everyday life.

The system described in this book covers the most effective techniques not only from the world of impromptu speaking, but also from acting, stand-up comedy, applied psychology and creative thinking.

Once you master the system, you will grow immensely as an impromptu speaker. Your audience members will think that what you do on stage, after such short preparation, is pure magic and will recall some of your speeches many years later.

After you master all of the magic components of the *Magic of Impromptu Speaking* system, your audiences will look forward to hearing you again and again during Q&A sessions, interviews, wedding receptions or contests.

Magic of Impromptu Speaking did wonders for me, it did wonders for everybody who learned it, and it will do wonders for you. Are you ready to begin a journey into the magic world of impromptu speaking? Let's go!

Best improvisation isn't improvisation

Imagine that you participate in a public speaking workshop. During the Q&A section, you ask the trainer, "John, can you please tell …?" And John answers with humor, interesting stories and great delivery techniques. The audience applauds. You think, "Wow. John is obviously an amazing impromptu speaker. I would never be able to answer a question off the cuff so well."

You might not know that John has conducted this workshop hundreds of times and answered your question more than once before. He tried different versions of the answer, analyzed various audience reactions and eventually chose the answer that got the best audience response.

Imagine that in the afternoon you turn on the TV and see a politician answering questions on a show. He sounds very smooth, confident and eloquent. You may think, "Wow, this politician really knows what he is talking about. He has a gift for speaking impromptu. I wish I could speak like he does."

You might not know, though, that the interview questions were sent in advance and that the politician has not only rehearsed and practiced the answers, but also rejected some of the questions.

Imagine that on Sunday night you go to see an improv show with your family. At the beginning of the show, one of the actors tells the audience, "Please shout out a random word. We will use it later in our performance." After getting the words, the improv actors sing a song or create funny sketches. You laugh through the entire evening and say, "These guys are so talented. I can't believe they just did that amazing show without any preparation."

What you might not know is that the group has practiced the same sketch with different words numerous times. Parts of the song and parts of the sketch are well rehearsed. Also, some people in the audience are friends of the actors and the words they shout are predetermined.

Does knowing this information make the improv show less exciting for you? No. Does the answer of the politician seem less professional? No. Does John the trainer sound less interesting? Of course not.

No matter how well you can think on your feet, a completely improvised answer can rarely be better than a prepared one. To get ready for impromptu speaking competitions, the contestants prepare and rehearse short blocks of the speech and stories that they can use in response to many different questions. Once they go on stage, they partially speak off the cuff and partially use the rehearsed blocks. The audience laughs, applauds and enjoys the speech. Everybody sees the end result. Few people know how the impressive impromptu speech is prepared.

Certainly, there are great shows, interviews and Q&A answers that are done completely off the cuff, but the best are always prepared, at least partially. To become a great impromptu speaker you need to learn how to eliminate the impromptu factor as much as possible.

Think about what questions may be asked during the Q&A section

While you prepare your speech at home, think about what questions the audience may ask. In most cases, you will be able to guess the questions and prepare the answers in advance. If you are giving the same speech many times, the questions from your audience members repeat themselves. Think about how you can answer each particular question you have heard before during the next Q&A section.

Discuss the interview questions in advance

If you are participating in a TV show or an interview, ask for questions that you will be asked so that your answers can be prepared in advance.

If you participate in a job interview, research common interview questions for candidates that are posted on the internet. Very often, they are shared on specialized forums and discussion boards by former job candidates who interviewed with the same company.

If you are invited to a birthday or a wedding

If you are invited to a birthday party or a wedding reception, you may be asked to give a toast. The best toasts are personal, so think of something specific about the person who has a birthday or is getting married and how you can personalize the toast.

Develop your impromptu speaking skills

The number of completely different questions that you can be asked is limited. After enough practice, it will be difictul for any question to surprise you. You will think, "Ah, I have been asked a similar question before, I'd answer it this way ..."

Many of the techniques you will learn later in Magic of Impromptu Speaking system will make you very effective at thinking on your feet. However, to make your improvisation on stage even more powerful, eliminate the impromptu factor as much as you can. The greatest impromptu speakers know that the best improvisation isn't improvisation.

The biggest secret of impromptu speaking

When I was about 12 years old, I had a huge fear. I was afraid of being beaten up by bullies in the street. I was so scared to go to school every day that my parents put me into the Kiokushin Karate school to get this fear out of me.

Every training session, after stretching and practicing punches, we had practice fights. I was fighting against, older, bigger and more experienced guys. It was painful, unpleasant and that time lasted an eternity for me.

One day our trainer, Alexander, said, "Please all sit in a circle. I have to tell you something." What he said not only changed my attitude to karate and fighting but also my attitude to impromptu speaking.

"Guys, don't fear the pain from the punches. Have an attitude to a fight as you would to a game. Here you missed a punch, here you managed to hit your opponent and there you made a successful block. It's fun! It's interesting, exciting and challenging!" These words struck a chord with me and I will remember them forever.

Once I started to think about the fight as a game, I forgot about the pain but instead enjoyed the challenge. My parents found it difficult to believe, but after 2 months I even volunteered to participate in the Kyiv city karate championship.

The fight lasted a minute and a half. I punched, kicked and made blocks, but most often I was punched. After 45 seconds, I felt completely exhausted, like I couldn't even raise my hands, much less punch. The audience raved, "Andrii! Andrii! Kick his ass! Kill him!" When you hear your name cheered, it should give you more strength and power to win, but in my case it was the opposite. Guess what? My opponent's name was also Andrii! He had a green belt and more than 7 years of experience in karate.

I lost that fight. I was beaten up. But it was truly fun! Few things can compare to it.

After the fight, the trainer called me and said, "Andrii, you fought like a lion. I am proud of you. And by the way, you really challenged greatly this guy who won two previous city championships." Those were the nicest words that I ever heard.

Was it painful to fight with the best karate fighter in Kyiv in full strength? Of course! Did I have bruises on my body after the fight? In fact, I had them almost everywhere. Was it fun? It was incredibly cool and this fight is one of my best childhood memories.

This karate championship had a tremendous effect on my development as a fighter, not only when sparring, but also in life. If you fight, your success is fully determined by your attitude. In impromptu speaking, it's the same. Your attitude fully determines your learning curve and success.

If you asked me, "Andrii, what is the most important technique to remember to become a world-class impromptu speaker?" I would say for sure, "Think about the impromptu speech as a game. Your attitude will change your frame of mind and instead of concentrating on the difficulty of finding the right words, your brain will deliver the perfect answer."

RELOCAte to a high-performance state

One day, while a student at the University of Michigan, I went to a bar with my friends and several alumni to celebrate the end of the school year. After we ordered drinks and started a conversation, I said something funny and everybody laughed. I told another joke and everybody laughed again. That afternoon the best comedians would have envied my ability to tell jokes on the spot, and for about 2 hours everyone was laughing really hard.

I often struggle to come up with a great joke, but that afternoon I couldn't stop the flow of amazing jokes coming to my mind.

Do you remember a time when you were much more effective than usual? The ideas were generated, the work was done quickly, your jokes were funny, and your impromptu speeches were great. This is a high-performance state. You have been in this state many times before and every time it felt like you were a rock star. What if you could be in this state during your next impromptu speech?

I have good news. You can get into a high-performance state quickly and whenever you want. The easiest way to get into this state is to use the RELOCAte technique developed by scientists who model and replicate behavior of successful people.

The research showed that in a high-performance state, people are relaxed, excited, lively, open and confident. The opposite is also true. If you become relaxed, excited, lively, open and confident simultaneously, you will get into the high-performance state and become dramatically more effective.

When actors play a role and want to convey a particular emotion of the character, they need to evoke it in themselves. They remember a situation from life when they felt this emotion clearly, relive it in their imagination and very soon begin to feel the emotion. This technique from the world of acting will help you with getting into the high-performance state.

To get into a high-performance state, you need to become simultaneously relaxed, excited, lively, open and confident. When these 5 states are combined, their individual effects on performance increase many times.

Relaxed

Relax all the muscles in your body completely except for the ones you need to stay upright. First, flex all your muscles and then quickly relax them. Relax all the muscles from your head to your feet. Pay attention to your breathing. Notice that each time you breathe and exhale, your body relaxes more and more until you are fully relaxed.

Excited

Remember a time in your life when you were really excited and relive this situation in your mind. Feel the excitement again. You are spontaneous and open for new opportunities and behaviors. Feel yourself excited and secure because your impromptu speech is just a game.

Lively

Become energetic. Feel the power within you and your readiness to do something. To become energetic, jump, dance, do physical exercise or just remember how it felt when you did something active. If you imagine it clearly enough, your nervous system won't notice any difference. Remember, however, that you need to build up your energy while staying completely relaxed. As soon as you notice tension – relax yourself. It might seem impossible to be lively and relaxed simultaneously, but it is easy. It's an amazing feeling of outside calmness and internal readiness.

Open

Remember a time when you were ready to accept anything that the world has to offer. You don't know what will happen in the next moment, but it is not important because you are ready to accept anything. Build up a feeling of openness until you can clearly feel it.

Confident

Recall a situation from your life when you felt absolutely confident in yourself. Maybe you said or did something you were 100% sure about. Relive it as clearly as you can and feel what you felt at that time. While building up a feeling of confidence, remain open, lively, excited and relaxed.

Again

Repeat again everything mentioned above! Every time you increase the intensity of each feeling, make sure you stay simultaneously relaxed, excited, lively, open and confident.

Go through this list several times and very soon you will get into a high-productivity state.

The high-productivity state will help you think quickly on your feet and create true impromptu magic on stage. I highly recommend getting into this state even when you give a prepared speech. It will allow you to be in the moment. It will allow you to improvise and make your speech special for your audience. RELOCAte is a very powerful technique that can get your impromptu speaking to the next level.

How to think on your feet

Stop internal dialogue

Numerous researches were conducted to compare the performance of our right brain (subconscious mind) and left brain (conscious mind). The results confirmed that our creative right brain is at least 2 million times faster than our analytical left brain.

Before you give an impromptu speech, there is usually very little time for preparation. As you can imagine, you need to think really fast. If you have less than 30 seconds to prepare an answer to a question, would you rather rely on your slow brain or your super-fast one?

If you want to become a world-class impromptu speaker and create speeches on the spot that will be remembered for years, your only choice is to use the creative super-fast brain as much as possible.

When an inexperienced impromptu speaker hears a question, he usually begins an internal dialogue, "Oh, I don't know what to say. No ... this won't be a perfect answer. What will everybody think about me? The time is passing so quickly and I still don't have any idea! Everybody will see my embarrassment and I will feel miserable."

When you speak to yourself, the internal dialogue blocks the super-fast creative brain and activates the analytical one. With such performance, it's impossible to think quickly and give a good answer.

To let your right brain and subconscious mind do their work, get rid of the internal dialogue. Don't let negative thoughts block your super-fast thinking. Once your brain is freed from the internal dialogue, it will process millions of options in a matter of seconds and will suggest the best possible answer to you. Just like anybody else, world-class speakers have the internal dialogue before the speech. The only difference is that they know exactly how to block it.

You may ask, "Andrii, how can I block the negative thoughts from popping up in my head and blocking my super-fast brain?"

To achieve this, you simply need to accept two beliefs of the world-class impromptu speaker: "I will definitely answer a question" and "I will not always have a stellar answer."

Once you make these two beliefs yours, nothing will stop your super fast brain from creating a perfect answer. Without an internal dialogue, you will grow immensely as an impromptu speaker and the quality of your speeches will be apparent.

Beliefs of the world-class impromptu speaker

I will definitely answer a question

Imagine that you are a boxer and when a fight begins, a thought pops up in your mind: "I don't have a clue how to begin a fight. What if everybody doesn't like my punches?"

These thoughts not only will block your instincts and super-fast brain, but also will bring you pain from the opponent's punch.

When you are in a ring, there is no time for internal dialogue and self-analysis. You first get into the fight and only then decide what to do with your body. You don't know whether you will win. You don't know exactly how you will block and punch. The only thing you know for sure is that you will definitely fight and your instincts will tell you what to do at each particular moment.

The moment you think, "My opponent looks scary," "I don't want to be beaten up really hard" or "What if he is stronger than I thought?" – you have already lost. The professional fighters know that and their belief is, "I first get into the fight and only then decide what to do with my body. My instincts and years of training will help me to decide what to do at each particular moment."

The same principle applies to impromptu public speaking. The most important attribute for any impromptu speaker is a "can-do" state of mind. Your subconscious mind will give you a perfect answer. However, to let it work you need to block all the negative thoughts first. Forget about thoughts like "I am unprepared" or "I am afraid" because no matter whether you know what to say or not, you will begin speaking.

The belief of the greatest impromptu speakers is the following: "Whether I have good ideas or not I will give an answer. My experience speaking impromptu and the techniques I learned in the past will help me to figure out the best answer to a question."

Once you stop considering whether to give an answer or not and what the consequences might be, the quality of your speeches will increase dramatically. All of your brainpower will be focused on figuring out an answer instead of judging your answer or deciding whether to speak or not. The question is not whether you will answer the question. The question is how you will answer it.

Later in this book, you will learn how to give an answer even if you didn't come up with a good idea. But for now, remember! You always answer the question and never block your super-fast creative brain with internal dialogue.

I won't always give a stellar answer

If you are Michael Jordan, you don't always score the basket, you just do it more often than other players. Just admit it. You will not always have a stellar impromptu answer no matter how well trained you are.

Depending on the question and situation, the quality of your answer will be different. Your worthiest answers may be better than the best answers of untrained speakers, but you need to accept the fact that not all your impromptu speeches will be stellar.

Everyone wants to give outstanding responses and receive standing ovations, but it just doesn't happen every time in impromptu speaking.

If you are worried about the quality of your answer, you begin thinking about the potential consequences of a poor answer. Self-analysis blocks your super-fast brain and leads to a guaranteed weak answer.

Just as Michael Jordan tries his best to make a shot, try to respond to the question the best you can. Don't worry about the quality of your answers. The sooner you accept the fact that not all your questions will be stellar, the sooner you will join the ranks of the world's best impromptu speakers.

Remember that impromptu speaking is just a game. No matter which answer you give, it is the best answer you could give in this particular situation and moment in time.

Accept the beliefs of the world-class impromptu speaker and your thinking speed on stage will increase at least 2 million times. Remember what the beliefs are? "I will not always give a stellar answer. I will begin speaking no matter what. My subconscious mind will suggest to me the best possible option for the answer at the moment I need it."

Yes and …

When you speak impromptu, time goes only forward and you can't change what you already said. If you say, "Oh, I am sorry. I didn't mean that" or "Forget about what I just said," it not only doesn't change what you just said but also makes your audience members think less of your speech.

They will think, "The speaker doesn't take what he is speaking about seriously and is wasting my time with meaningless excuses."

Imagine that after hearing a question, "Which animal is your favorite pet?" you respond, "I love dogs. When I was 7 years old my mom bought me a puppy, which I named Chip." At this moment, you remember a funny story about your friend's cat and want to change your response completely.

You may think, "What can I do in such a situation?" The most important thing is to accept what you said before and move forward. What you already said is a done deal and was important at the time you said it. Never apologize or say it was unimportant.

Make a quick transition from "dogs" to "cats" and continue your speech in a new direction. For example, "Dogs were truly my favorite pets until recently. A month ago my friend Jim said, 'Andrii, I am going to Hawaii for vacation. Can you please look after my kitten for 2 weeks?'" Next, I would tell my story and make a conclusion stating that cats are my favorite pets. With such a transition, your answer is very smooth and what you said about dogs sounds very naturally integrated into the overall response.

During an impromptu speech, you may change the direction of your answer several times, but make sure that you don't reject what you said earlier. Tell yourself, "Yes, I agree with everything said before and can continue my speech in any direction." You can switch easily between ideas using transitions and your speech will sound natural.

The rule of the first thought

The rule of the first thought says, "Once you hear a question, begin answering it based on the first idea that pops up in your head."

If you wait longer, your internal dialogue will turn on. You will think, "I can't figure out the best answer. This idea is not perfect. What will everybody think about me? Oh, the time is passing and I still don't know what to say." Internal dialogue will block your subconscious and activate slow analytical thinking. Eventually, it almost always will lead you to a poor impromptu answer.

By answering with your first thought, you block the conscious thinking and activate the subconscious super-fast idea generation.

Before you begin speaking, it is not necessary to come up with the entire answer. As a minimum, you only need a starting point. Answer based on the first thought and if you come up with a good idea later, it is always possible to change direction of your speech on the fly.

How do I find time for thinking?

The first 30 seconds

After you hear a question, always take 30 seconds to think about the answer. Not only will your reply appear thoughtful, but you also will let your subconscious mind process millions of ideas for the answer. This habit will make all your impromptu speeches significantly better.

Many speakers are afraid of speaking impromptu. They think, "I doubt that I will come up with a great answer within only 30 seconds."

You see, it is indeed difficult to come up with a great answer within only 30 seconds even for the world's best impromptu speakers. If you know the entire answer after you hear a question, that's great, but it might not happen every time. In fact, you have much more time than 30 seconds to think.

Remember that it's not mandatory to know the entire answer when you begin speaking. What you need to know is only a starting point, a first thought. You will have plenty of time to think about the rest of your answer later.

Think while you speak

The speed of your thinking is much faster than your speed of talking. While you talk about an idea, your brain generates new thoughts that will allow you to develop the idea you are talking about, or transition to another one.

When you are talking with your friend about the amazing food at the sea resort where you vacationed, a thought may pop into your head about something funny that happened during the tour to the waterfalls. You transition smoothly from talking about the food at the resort to telling the story about the tour. For your friend it sounds completely natural, and he or she might not know that the thought about the story came to your mind only a few seconds ago.

The same principle is highly applicable in impromptu speaking. When you talk about an idea, your creative brain is thinking really quickly and, depending on what thoughts come to your mind, you develop a current idea or transition to another one.

The best time for thinking is while you are talking because it is not limited. You can slow down the rate of your speech to give you even more time to think.

If you feel that you don't know what to speak about, just take a pause. A dramatic pause is totally acceptable. During a short pause, your brain will catch up and your audience won't even notice anything unusual.

Remember that your brain is many times faster than your words. While you talk, your brain is thinking about what to say next. If you feel that you need more time to think, just speak more slowly or pause.

Exercises for thinking on your feet

Exercise 1: Flow of consciousness

The goal of this exercise is to develop the ability to begin a speech on any topic at any place. If you are sitting in a room, driving a car or walking somewhere, just talk about everything you see, feel and think.

For example, as I am writing these lines I am sitting in New York's JFK airport waiting for my flight. Here is how a flow of consciousness may look to me: "Now I sit on a metal bench in the New York airport. In front of me I see a man that speaks Russian on the phone. He is probably speaking to his wife. There are about 5 hours before my flight. I will probably continue writing a book about impromptu speaking for another hour or two and then will look for a place to have lunch. Oh, why aren't there any outlets in the airport for passengers? My laptop battery will be completely discharged soon. Actually, I am very excited about my flight to Europe. Every time I fly anywhere I feel like the plane takes me to a completely different world with new acquaintances, new adventures and new life experiences."

Certainly, I can't call the last paragraph a great impromptu speech; however, it took me literally 0 seconds to create it, because I just wrote what came to my mind. The goal here is to forget about the content of your speech and just fill 2-3 minutes of time with your flow of consciousness.

This is perhaps one of the most important exercises in the entire book. Once you are able to consistently fill 2-3 minutes with flow of consciousness, you can give an impromptu speech on any topic.

Everything else you learn in this book will help you to make your speech effective, interesting and valuable. However, at this point it is very important to gain confidence that no matter what the question is you can always find words for the answer.

When you experience a tough situation in finding what to say, just say what you really are thinking about. The audience loves speakers who show their vulnerability and tell the truth. Be sincere and just say what is going through your mind.

Imagine that you are asked a question, "If you could make only one wish and you knew it would come true, what would it be and why?"

Using the skills acquired in the "flow of consciousness" exercise, I might start with the following, "Once I heard a question I almost answered with, 'I want peace everywhere in the world.' If I said that, I believe you guys would think well of me. But my inner voice screamed, 'I want a billion dollars. Oh, better yet I want to become the mayor of a city like New York.'

At the age of 22, I went through a leadership training course and one of the tasks was to get at least 50 signatures from unknown people on the street. After I got probably 20 signatures, I saw two 20-year-old girls sitting on a bench. I said, 'I plan to become the mayor of Kyiv and need to gather 100,000 signatures to participate in the elections. Would you sign here, please?' The response I got knocked me down and I still remember it. 'Are you kidding me? You will never become a mayor.'"

You see, I didn't know how to answer the question in the beginning, so I said what was on my mind. However, a few moments later the story about collecting signatures popped into my head and I transitioned to that story.

Sometimes a theme will come readily to your mind and you can simply introduce the topic, give your view on it, and proceed to building a speech. However, at other times you may not have any idea about how best to answer a question. In such a case just say what you think until you come up with an idea about what to speak about. Keep your mind focused on the thoughts and concepts that arise in your head. You will see new relationships among ideas and concepts as you speak.

Even if the thoughts you say out loud are not phenomenal, your audience might be much more interested in hearing them rather than apologies or filler words.

Exercise 2: Talk about an object for 5 minutes

The goal of the "talk about an object" exercise is to develop ease in associative speech. First, pick any object you see. Second, talk about this object to your partner for about 5 minutes. Describe its history, functions and applications, and say what you think about it. After some time, you will realize that you can speak for several minutes about any object. This skill will help you significantly in impromptu speaking.

Decide which question to answer

Every day we are asked dozens of questions that we answer directly. For example, "Andrii, do you want tea or coffee for breakfast?" "I would prefer tea," or "Andrii, what time is it now?" "It's half past eight." We are so used to giving direct answers that when we hear a question from the audience we tend to answer it directly because we think that it is the only option.

No one can force you to answer a particular question. Only you can decide what answer to give or whether to answer it at all. The possibilities are endless: you can answer a question directly, answer only part of the question, make a speech that has no relationship to the question, say "no comment" or just decide to answer later.

Great impromptu speakers are aware of all the options. If they answer a question directly, it is because they made a conscious decision to do so, not because they think it is the only option. If you want to grow as an impromptu speaker, you need to accept that there are no limitations for your speech. Your answer does not have to be clever, truthful, realistic or related to the question. The only rule is that you need to make a conscious decision about what question you are going to answer.

Imagine that you are asked, "If you could vote for the most outstanding person of the 20th century, who would you vote for and why?"

What are the first thoughts that pop up in your head? Most people instantly think about somebody famous they know from the 20th century and try to explain logically why this person is the most outstanding.

Be aware that there are many more directions for your answer and you need to make a conscious decision about your direction. Below you can find some of the options for your choice of the question.

Answer a question as you understand it

Very often a question is asked obscurely. For example, in the question, "If you could vote for the most outstanding person of the 20th century, who would you vote for and why?" the definition of an "outstanding person" is quite obscure.

For some people, this may be the person who came up with the greatest invention; for others, it may be the funniest comedian. You can handle such a question by defining how you understand it and then answering a question in your interpretation.

For example, "For me, the most outstanding person of the 20th century is the person who had the biggest impact on my life and without whom my life simply wouldn't be possible. It's my grandmother …"

First, you define what the most outstanding person means to you, then you give a speech about your grandmother.

Once you are asked a question with obscure terms, you might be tempted to think hard about what the questioner really meant. However, it is not important. Just explain how you understand the question and answer it as you understood it.

Pick a word from a context

"If you could vote for the most outstanding person of the 20th century, who would you vote for and why?" Take any word from the text of the question and talk about it.

For example, if you chose the word "vote" your answer might be, "When we try to decide who the most outstanding person in the 20th century is, or who the best candidate to become a president is, we vote. But is public voting the best way to make a selection?" Then you can talk about voting and alternative ways to make a decision. In this method, you can pick any word from the question and make a speech about it.

Answer any question you want

With a proper transition, you can give an answer to any question of your choice regardless of the question asked.

For example, "Andrii, if you could vote for the most outstanding person of the 20th century, who would you vote for and why?"

I can make a transition like "What is important today is not who the most outstanding person in the 20th century was, but, rather, if the current school education system will help our children to make the 21st century even more remarkable than the 20th" or "This reminds me of a conversation with my dad when I was 7 about who I wanted to become when I grow up."

If you use an appropriate transition you can literally, with one or two sentences, get to any topic you really want to talk about. Regardless of the original question, you can answer any question using this technique. Politicians use this technique during interviews and TV shows all the time.

Answer a part of the question

Imagine that you are asked, "Do you agree with the following quote by Max De Pree, 'The first responsibility of a leader is to define reality. The last is to say thank you. In between, the leader is a servant.'?"

You can just pick any part of the question you liked and answer it. For example, you could answer the question, "Do you agree that the leader is a servant?" Or, you could instead answer the question, "Do you agree that the first responsibility of a leader is to define reality?" It's not always mandatory to answer the question completely; you can decide just to answer partially.

As you can see, answering a question directly is only one option. Be aware that there are numerous other options and you can be creative in choosing a question for your impromptu speech. Remember, your only goal should be to choose a question consciously and give a valuable answer to your audience. If you feel that slightly altering a question will help you to deliver a more valuable answer to the audience and to change their perspective, do so.

Transitions

When giving an impromptu speech, you talk about your first idea, then transition to the second idea and talk about it, then you transition to the third one and so on. To make your speech sound smooth, you use special sentences that help to move from one idea to another. If you master transitions you will not only be able to go smoothly from one thought to another in your speech, but you also will be able to talk about any topic for hours without preparation.

If you want to take your impromptu speaking to the next level and create smooth transitions on your feet, you need to practice. The exercises below will help to dramatically improve your ability to create smooth transitions in impromptu speech.

Exercises for transitions

You can work on any exercises in this book with a partner or on your own. The exercises are very similar to what you will experience while speaking off the cuff in front of the audience. You should focus on one particular element at a time. The more you practice, the easier it will be for you to speak impromptu and the more fun you will have on stage.

Exercise 1: Linguistic pyramids

The goal of this exercise is to develop a skill of making quick analogies and generalizations.

Pick any object that you can see, for example a cup. An object can either be generalized to the higher class or be split into subclasses. The higher class for a cup is dishes. Dishes may include plates, glasses or bowls.

Let's split a cup into several different subtypes. For example, there can be a coffee cup, a teacup, an aluminum cup or a porcelain cup.

Now pick different objects and play with raising or lowering the class. Devote about 5 minutes to this exercise. It's enough time to improve a skill, but not get bored. Do you want to learn how linguistic pyramids can help during your next impromptu speech?

Imagine that a topic for your impromptu speech is a cup. Here is how you can answer: "There are cups made from glass, porcelain or aluminum. The most special for me are cups made from aluminum because they remind me of my trip to China, which is a world leader in aluminum production."

Or you can answer, "A cup is a dish from which it is very convenient to drink coffee or tea. When I was a kid I wished that all dishes were made from paper because it was my responsibility to wash dishes after a meal."

In the first example, we transitioned with the help of lowering a class from a cup to the trip to China. In the second example, we transitioned from a cup to responsibilities by generalizing. "Linguistic pyramids" is a great exercise that can help you to transition from any object to the idea or topic you want to talk about.

Exercise 2: How a donkey is similar to a table

The goal of this exercise is to learn how to create analogies between completely unrelated objects. First, pick an animate being and an inanimate object. Then explain how this animate being is similar to the inanimate object.

For example, both a donkey and a table have 4 legs. You can sit on a donkey and on a table. It's difficult to move both a stubborn donkey and a heavy table. Both a donkey and a table can't speak English. A farmer can own both a table and a donkey.

Pick several pairs of animate beings and inanimate objects and explain how they are similar as in the example above. Do this exercise for 5 minutes.

Exercise 3: Creative associations

Choose any object or term and explain what it associates with in your mind. For example, if I were doing this exercise, it might look like the following: money-banker, coffee-mother or vacation-beach. Don't spend too much time thinking. The first association that comes to your mind is the best one.

Let's see how it could be used in the impromptu speech, "When I think about coffee, I remember my mother because she makes the best coffee I have ever drunk." With such a transition, you can easily change a topic from coffee to your mother or mothers in general.

Or "I associate peace with beauty pageants because the contestants often say, 'My biggest dream is world peace.' I believe they say it because the judges like it and it gives them a better chance to win the pageant. What if everyone always told the truth? Would the world be a better place?"

With this transition, I moved from "peace" to a question, "Would the world be a better place if everyone told only the truth?" Now your entire impromptu speech can answer this question and it will sound very logical because of the transition.

Structure of the impromptu speech

Many speakers follow a structure while giving a prepared speech but speak without any plan at all during the Q&A section. If your speech doesn't have a structure, your listeners may get lost. If they get lost, they get irritated and stop listening.

All great speeches have the same structure: opening, body and conclusion. You can improvise within these 3 components; however, the basic structure is always fixed. Nevertheless, your off-the-cuff speech is unprepared so be creative within a basic structure.

Opening

The main purpose of the opening is to get the attention of the audience and to give a flavor of what to expect. There are numerous ways to begin an impromptu speech; however, below you can find 3 methods that have proven to be most effective.

Begin with a statement

You can begin a speech with a statement on your position or a startling statement. For example, "At the age of 9, I wanted to become a dancer. At the age of 19, I became a networking engineer. At the age of 26, I will become a dancer." The unusual statement draws the attention of the audience and gives a hint about the direction of your speech.

Start with a call back

A very powerful way to begin an impromptu speech is to call back to the common experience of the entire audience. Mention what a previous speaker said, an event that recently happened in the audience, or refer to a person who everyone in the audience knows.

Call backs make your speech very personal and special for the audience. People feel that your impromptu speech is just for them. Every time you use a call back, you may notice the reaction of the audience. It is so powerful that the audience almost always reacts.

Start with a story

Everyone loves hearing stories in movies, in reality shows or in speeches. When you hear a story, you can relive an episode from the life of its characters. When you begin a speech with a story, such an opening captures the audience members' attention and introduces them not only to your speech but also to the world of your story's characters.

For example, "Two years ago my college friend John called me and said ..." or "Last summer, in London, I was invited to a Christmas party. That evening completely changed my attitude toward Argentine tango."

I am often asked, "Andrii, is the opening and conclusion any different in an impromptu speech compared with a prepared speech?"

Yes. Because an impromptu speech usually lasts 1-3 minutes, its components are significantly shorter than in a prepared speech. For example, an introduction and a conclusion may sometimes be only 1 sentence long. Because you think while you speak and may change the direction of your speech in the middle, occasionally the opening may have little relation to the rest of the speech, but the conclusion should always be relevant, strong and clear.

Body of the speech

In the body of your impromptu speech, always share a single point. Because the impromptu speech is usually really short, you can convey only one point effectively. If you try to convey 2 or more points, it's impossible to make a solid answer. You can convey other messages while answering further questions during the interview or a Q&A session. The more focused your answer, the stronger it is.

There are different strategies that impromptu speakers use to answer a question, but there are 3 frameworks that have proven to be the most effective. These frameworks are consistently used by the world's best impromptu speakers. Even if you answer questions using only these 3 frameworks, all your unprepared speeches will be at a very good level.

Conclusion

Conclusion is perhaps the most important part of the entire speech because what is said in the end is remembered best by the audience. If your speech is good, the last sentence is what your listeners will recite to their friends later.

Finish your speech with a statement and your audience will remember your point. Finish your speech with a call to action and your audience may do something differently after your speech. These are the two most commonly used ways to end a speech, and both have been proven effective for powerful impromptu speeches.

A conclusion needs to summarize the takeaway message of the speech and restate your point. The purpose of speaking impromptu is not to fill time, but to give value to the audience and share your unique perspective on the question. Don't hide behind clever and meaningless words. Any good off-the-cuff speech needs to have a clear point to be effective.

To be clear, your point needs to be less than 15 words long and should include a message that you want your audience to remember if they forget everything else you said. If your takeaway message is longer than 15 words, it is not clear for you, and if it's not clear for you there is no chance it will be clear for your audience.

One more thing … Look for an elegant way to tie the conclusion to the beginning of the speech. If you manage to do so, your speech will sound solid and consistent.

3 magic impromptu speaking frameworks

If you are a general and lead an army into combat, you need to have a good strategy. During the actual battle, a lot can happen unexpectedly and you will have to make many decisions impromptu. If you make some bad decisions during the fight, you can still win, but if you don't have any strategy before the fight begins, it is almost impossible to win even with a great army. The same is true for impromptu speaking. If you want your answer to be world-class, you need to have a strategy for your speech.

Having analyzed thousands of great impromptu speakers, I figured out that the best impromptu speeches in all kinds of situations were constructed using the same 3 approaches. These 3 effective strategies were included in *Magic of Impromptu Speaking* system and work 100% of the time. They are different and are used in different cases, but all of them are essential for you to know as an impromptu speaker.

Tell a story

Do you remember the tale *Little Red Riding Hood* that you heard in childhood? Do you remember any PowerPoint presentation that you heard several years ago?

The reason why most of us remember the tale about *Little Red Riding Hood* but don't remember dry PowerPoint presentations lies in the secret of how our memory works.

People remember points of wisdom only when they are associated with stories that happened to them or that they have heard.

When we hear a story we can imagine a beach where the action takes place, hear how the characters talk and feel the emotions. Stories are easy to remember for a human brain as they evoke emotions and activate visual, auditory and kinesthetic senses.

If you tell a fact or make a point that is associated with a story, it may be remembered forever. If your points are very clever and interesting but are not associated with a story or a visual example, they may be forgotten right after you finish speaking.

Even a story that is not spectacular, well told or long can have a dramatic effect on how your point is remembered. Our brains remember information only in association with stories, visual examples or personal experiences.

Three years ago, I heard a story told by a woman over the phone during a webinar. The story was about a time when she worked as a nurse in a hospital while her city was bombarded during a war.

Vocal variety was far from great. There wasn't any conflict or clear conclusion, but even after several years, I can still retell this story in detail.

An inexperienced speaker who is making his or her first speech by telling a story is much more effective on stage than an experienced speaker who doesn't. This is how powerful stories are. If you remember just one thing from this book, I want it to be this: "Tell a story and associate it with a point."

In impromptu speaking, just as in prepared speaking, the most effective strategy is to tell a story and make a point. The best structure you can use on stage for the impromptu speech is opening, story and conclusion.

Stories help to eliminate the unexpectedness factor. The story happened in your life, you may have told it before, and while you are telling it on stage, you clearly know what the next sentence is. While your brain is freed from thinking about the next sentence, you can focus on pondering the conclusion.

Transition to a story from your life

Sometimes you can answer a question directly with one of the stories from your life. For example, "Please tell me about your first day of school." You can easily answer by telling a story about your first day of school.

However, very often you need a transition to go smoothly from the question that was asked to one of the stories that you remember.

When my wife and I lived in Santa Clara, California, I was a member of 7 Toastmasters clubs and visited many others as a guest. Toastmasters is an organization that gives speakers the opportunity to practice prepared and impromptu speeches in front of a live audience.

During one of the club meetings, I said to my wife, "Olena, let's bet that no matter what question is asked I can always answer it with the same story." That week I answered 7 different questions with the same story but different transitions.

If you have a certain amount of stories that you remember, you can transition to them from almost any question using phrases like, "This reminds me of" or "What is important today." Politicians often use a transition technique. They are asked different questions but with the help of a transition, they come to the topic they want to talk about.

Craft a fictional story on the go

Create an imaginary story to support your point. There is no limit to how creative you can be. You can say, "Imagine that" or "What if …" and let your imagination go wild. Some of the best impromptu speeches I have ever heard used this approach. Try it. It's extremely effective and fun. Audiences love it.

For example, your speech may begin with, "I have never gone fishing, but I imagine that …" Let your audience know that your imagination went wild and tell a tall tale. You don't necessarily need to tell the truth.

When you need to answer a question during a corporate meeting, you occasionally may find that telling a story is not appropriate. Sometimes you may decide to go with an easier approach than telling a story. For these situations, there are 2 other frameworks in the *Magic of Impromptu Speaking* system that you may find very handy.

PEEP

PEEP (Point, Explanation, Example and Point) is a very easy but effective and practical approach. If you struggle with finding an appropriate story for the answer, you can use this method. Use it when you need to give an opinion and back it up.

Point: Make a point in the opening of your speech.

Explanation: State your reasons for making this point in the body of the speech.

Example: Use an example or illustration to justify your previous remarks. Use words like "for example" or "imagine." Speaking about personal experiences will make your answer genuine and also memorable for your audience members.

Point: Drive home your point again. Link the conclusion to the opening.

As you can see, the first and the last "P" in PEEP serve as opening and conclusion. Explanation and Example fill the body of the speech. Example makes your point of view real and understandable for your listeners because just like a story, it activates the audience's senses in imagination. This approach is very popular among many impromptu speakers because it is very easy to apply.

Position, Action, Benefit

The Position, Action, Benefit approach is very useful when you report your findings to the board of directors or make a sales pitch to a CEO who has only 5 minutes to listen. I call this approach corporate because it is best suited for the corporate setting where telling a story might not always be appropriate and the decision needs to be made quickly. Your answer might not be remembered for years, but it will allow your audience to make an informed decision quickly.

For example, you may be asked, "Should we buy this company or not?", "How can your product help us?" or "Should we stop this project or continue it?"

Position: State your position on the question asked.

Action: Tell which action needs to be taken to implement your suggestion.

Benefit: Describe the benefit of your position.

If you answer a question using the position, action, benefit approach, your audience members will have all the information they need to make a decision.

Storytelling

Stories engage visual, auditory and kinesthetic senses of the audience. The day after your impromptu answer, the listeners won't remember any words you said; they will remember only what they saw, heard and felt in their imagination while you were speaking.

If you want your point to be remembered and have any impact, you need to associate it with a story or visual example. You may think, "Andrii, how can I tell an effective story that the audience will remember and enjoy?" You have told numerous stories to your family or friends about your vacation or what happened at work; however, for speaking impromptu effectively you need to learn the 3 foundations of storytelling.

Details tell a story

Stories are effective because they create scenes in the imagination of the audience. Use details to make the scenes real for your listeners.

Imagine that a speaker says, "I lost the first fight in a karate competition, but I enjoyed the experience." Is this phrase interesting for you? Is it memorable? Did it make you imagine the story?

Recall a final climax scene in a story, "The biggest secret of impromptu speaking."

"The fight lasted a minute and a half. I punched, kicked and made blocks, but most often I was punched. After 45 seconds I felt completely exhausted, like I couldn't even raise my hands, much less punch. The audience raved, "Andrii! Andrii! Kick his ass! Kill him!" When you hear your name cheered, it should give you more strength and power to win, but in my case it was the opposite. Guess what? My opponent's name was also Andrii! He had a green belt and more than 7 years of experience in karate. I lost that fight. I was beaten up. But it was truly fun! Few things can compare to it."

The second description of the same fight gives you much more detail. You know the background of my opponent in karate, who the audience supported, how long the fight lasted and how I felt during the fight. All these details make a story memorable. You will forget the words but will remember the scene that was drawn into the imagination by these words.

Details are the most important component of any story. Tell stories and make them detail-rich. This principle will make you a really good impromptu speaker. People like stories. People like details. People love speakers who know it.

Dialogue

If you don't use dialogue in a presentation, it's a news report, an article, a narration, but not a speech. Dialogue is an essential component of any story as it brings events of the past to life.

For example, "When I came home, I went to the kitchen, took several sheets of paper from my bag and started working on the problem. My reputation at school was at stake. At 1 a.m. my mom said, "Andrii, it's late. Go to bed. How is it going with that math problem, by the way?" "Mom, I see why nobody solved it before. It's insanely difficult. I tried everything and now have run out of ideas." This event happened many years ago, but a dialogue brings it alive and the audience can see how the story unfolds in real time.

All world-class impromptu speakers use dialogues in their speeches because they know that dialogue is a magical tool that makes a speech engaging, real, and memorable.

Every story is a combination of narration and dialogue, and your goal, as a speaker, is to find the right proportion. Most speakers have too little dialogue and too much narration in their impromptu speeches, so if you want to make your story engaging and memorable just increase the amount of dialogue in it. Dialogue is what turns an okay speech into an outstanding one.

Conflict

Conflict is a barrier between a character and what he or she wants to achieve. Conflict introduces an intrigue to a story and creates questions in the minds of the audience members. People are interested in hearing your story because they want to learn how the conflict will be resolved.

The structure of a story is introduction of the conflict, escalation of the conflict, and the resolution. As the impromptu speech is much shorter than a prepared one, you need to introduce a conflict very early, often in the first couple of sentences.

For example, "When I was about 12 years old, I had a huge fear. I was scared of being beaten up on the street by bullies. I was so afraid to go to school every day that my parents enrolled me in the Kiokushin Karate school to get this fear out of me."

Conflict can be a battle of man versus man, man versus difficulties, or even man versus himself. In this example, it is a battle of me against my fear.

Even if you use dialogue and details, the audience can still get bored listening to your speech without a conflict. Every great story, like a Hollywood movie, needs to have a conflict in the beginning that will be resolved later.

To make your story a blockbuster, introduce a conflict early in a story. Escalate it and once your audience is eager to know how it gets resolved, show the climax and give a resolution.

Your goal is to try to adhere to 3 fundamentals of the perfect story. Keep them in mind before you go on stage and you will notice how engaging your stories become for the listeners. Your audience members will think, "Wow! It is pure magic how this speaker can craft such outstanding stories after only 30 seconds of preparation." You, however, will know that this magic consists of 3 words: details, dialogue and conflict.

Exercises for storytelling

To become a well-rounded impromptu speaker you need to master the skill of telling stories. In impromptu speaking, you need to think really fast and decide how your story will unfold while you are telling it. As with any other skill, mastery in telling stories impromptu comes with practice. "Story-story," "nouns from the bag" and "complete a story" are excellent games that will polish your skill of telling stories while you have fun with friends or fellow impromptu speakers.

Exercise 1: Story-story

The goal of the "story-story" game is to develop a skill of talking about any topic. A moderator provides a setting for a story. He or she points at a person who begins telling a story. The moderator gives a signal to one of the participants and he or she continues the story from the place where the previous person stopped.

The new person picks up from the last word and tries to continue the narrative. Every speaker should have several turns to add to a story. Usually a moderator suggests when a story ends and asks one of the participants to make a conclusion.

Exercise 2: Nouns from the bag

In this exercise, participants write nouns on a slip of paper. Proper nouns are acceptable. In fact, the stranger the nouns, the more interesting this game will be.

After all the papers have been collected in a bag, one participant begins telling a story. After a storyline is established, the moderator picks a paper from the bag and a speaker includes this word in a story. For example, "Yesterday I went to a restaurant with my wife. It was our wedding anniversary and I wanted to make this afternoon special for us."

At this point the moderator picks the word "penguin" from the bag and a speaker continues the story. "The restaurant is called 'Antarctica' and they had a special dish of the day made from the meat of penguin. So I ordered it for both of us. I asked, 'Honey, do you remember how we met 10 years ago?'" Now the moderator picks another word from the bag and this continues until the story ends.

The game "nouns from the bag" develops on-the-spot thinking and the skill of crafting a story while you speak. As you can see, this exercise is very similar to what you face during the actual impromptu speech. You tell a story impromptu and every few seconds decide in which direction it will go.

Exercise 3: Complete a story

This exercise helps to develop the ability to craft an imaginary story with any setting. A participant should tell a story in the setting that the moderator announces.

For example:

"I received an anonymous text that said, 'I know where you are …'"

"The trail dead-ended into dense forest. A sign read, 'Enter at your own risk …'"

"While walking to the store I found an envelope. Inside was $10,000. I decided to …"

"A laid-back bike ride through the wilderness turned dangerous when out of nowhere jumped …"

"A knock on the passenger side window was startling. When I looked to see who it was …"

"The rain didn't show signs of stopping, but I had to …"

"It was the second time they called. This time I answered …"

You can play this game with only one partner or in a large group. Invent interesting introductions and let your imagination go wild. The more freedom you allow your imagination during the practice, the more it will help you later in impromptu speaking.

Take a stand

Take a stand. You need to have your particular point of view about a question asked. Imagine that you sit in the audience and a politician is asked a question, "Could you please tell us when we will get out of the economic crisis?"

A speaker answers, "It depends. If the government takes the right actions, we might get out of this crisis relatively quickly. However, if our nation doesn't unite and the government doesn't take the right steps to eliminate economic problems, the crisis may last much longer."

Neither answer gives any value nor will it be remembered or cited by the media. However, suppose the politician says, "I think that in 3 years we should get to the point of 2008 in our economy." Even if it's only an opinion that is not backed up by any data, it gives value, it will be cited by the news media, and it might be remembered for a long time.

One of the common mistakes that some speakers make is rattling off whatever comes to mind simply to fill up the time without making a stand. A good speech always has a message and a definitive point of view. Never be on the fence and never say "it depends."

Delivery techniques

Many speakers, after hearing a question, think, "Oh, the most important thing for me is to figure out what to say." How you deliver an impromptu speech, however, is much more important than what you say.

Be genuine

If you asked me, "What is the most powerful delivery technique in impromptu speaking?" I would say "Sincerity, for sure!" Many people want to be liked by the audience and play a role on stage. They want to show that they are knowledgeable like a Harvard professor, eloquent like Tony Robbins and charismatic like Steve Jobs.

The audience can see much more than you can only imagine through your nonverbal signals. Once your listeners feel that you are not genuine, they will stop trusting you and your speech will be over for them.

The audience members don't need another Tony Robbins, Steve Jobs or Martin Luther King. They need you. People will forgive anything on stage except insincerity. If you are truly genuine, your speech will be perceived well even if you mess up everything else.

Sometimes my students ask me, "Andrii, I want to be genuine on stage, but I don't know how. Is there any technique that can help me?"

You can't be genuine without perceiving your audience members as your best friends, without having fun speaking impromptu, and without intending to give value. There is a magical invocation that will ensure that your impromptu speech is always genuine and effective. It always works for me, for my students, for great impromptu speakers and for everybody who uses it. However, to make it work you need to truly believe in it. Before you go on stage repeat the following words, "*I will have fun from speaking impromptu and will enjoy every second of being on stage. People in the audience are the best people in my life. They are as important to me as my family or best friend. The only reason I am on stage is to give value and change the lives of my audience members for the better.*"

Be energetic

Many years ago I attended an acting training led by a famous stage director. One of the students in my group was 21-year-old Julie. One day the trainer said, "Now it's time to give a 3-minute speech that you have been working on during the weekend. Julie, you are first." When Julie went on stage she smiled and said, "The title of my speech is 'Fashion trends of spring.' This season, the polka-dot dress is popular. I like the bright colors …"

I thought, "It's amazing! Julie didn't implement anything that the stage director taught us. Her speech doesn't have any structure, she stumbles a lot, the topic is not interesting for me, but her speech is awesome! I could listen to it for hours!"

I asked myself, "What is special about her speech?" And then I realized, "Julie is highly energetic and passionate about what she is talking about and it's contagious." This is perhaps one of the most valuable lessons I learned about public speaking in my life.

If you are passionate about your topic, your energy is contagious and very soon everyone in the audience will be excited. They will think, "Wow, there could be something special about this topic since the speaker is that excited. I should listen." On the other hand, if the audience members see that you are indifferent, they will become bored and indifferent, just like you.

Being energetic is one of the foundations of the successful impromptu speech. No matter what you are talking about impromptu, be excited about it and speak with energy and passion. When the energy of excitement spreads throughout the room it's magic and you are the wizard.

Gestures

When you look at some beginner impromptu speakers, you may notice that they occasionally stare at the ceiling or make nervous gestures. Why? The brain is busy figuring out what to say and a speaker tends to forget completely about gestures and eye contact.

When you are on stage, you might think that the biggest problem is to find the right words because the audience might judge your speech based on what you say. However, the audience also judges your speech based on what you do on stage while you are thinking or speaking. If you are fidgeting with your fingers, dancing from one leg to another or staring at the ceiling, it not only looks irritating, but also makes your listeners doubt your confidence in what you say.

The expectations for gestures and movements on stage are usually lower for impromptu than for a prepared speech, but you need to adhere to some basic best practices.

Just like in a prepared speech, all your gestures should be broad and open. You should always look directly into the eyes of one of the audience members and of course avoid all kinds of nervous gestures.

You may think, "How can I control so many things on stage? I should think about what to say, control my eye contact, movements and gestures. Isn't it too much?" The answer to this question relates to the foundation of thinking on your feet.

If you try to think consciously about your content, gestures, eye contact and movements, you will easily get overwhelmed. Your goal is to not think about all these things! Your goal is to trust your super-fast subconscious mind.

If you asked me, "How do you control your gestures?" I would say, "They just happen. I trust my subconscious and it gives me signals of when to gesture and how to gesture. The same happens when you walk. Your subconscious gives you a signal when to make a movement and you make it without thinking."

When you practice speaking impromptu at a Toastmasters club or in a circle of friends, ask whether you make any kind of irritating gestures and whether you make proper eye contact. Eliminate the mistakes one by one in your subsequent speeches. After a certain amount of practice all your gestures, movements and nonverbal signals will be good even without thinking about them.

Fear of impromptu speaking

I have interviewed more than 100 speakers and all of them have said that they do feel fear of speaking impromptu. I asked, "Is there anything particular that you fear?" and received the following responses, "I fear that I will not be able to create a great answer quickly" and "I am afraid that the audience will not like my answer and will think badly of me." In fact, all speakers, to a certain degree, fear speaking impromptu. It is easy to reduce fear of impromptu speaking significantly if you follow the 3 recommendations below.

Rely on your previous experience

If you fear impromptu speaking, you are not alone. People fear everything that is unfamiliar to them. Every time you get out of your comfort zone you feel fear, but it is also the time you grow the most.

When I was 7 my mom said, "Starting Monday you will go to school on your own." I said, "Mom, I am very afraid to go to school without you. I haven't gone anywhere by myself before. I am afraid that I will get lost."

Guess what? I felt fear only the first day I went to school without Mom. However, I then realized that I did remember the path, I had gone to school already many times before, and there was nothing to fear. The same happens to every impromptu speaker.

After you give more than a dozen answers impromptu and practice the techniques of thinking on your feet, you will think, "Hey, I have spoken impromptu before! Sometimes my answers were great, sometimes they were so-so, but it wasn't as bad as I feared. The audience didn't eat me alive and I even had fun."

To reduce fear of impromptu speaking, just make it familiar to you and it will become a part of your comfort zone. Speak impromptu as often as you can and after a while you will not fear it anymore. Why? Because you already spoke impromptu and know from your previous experience that there is nothing to fear.

Accept that not every answer will be stellar

Realize and accept the fact that not all of your impromptu answers will be stellar. Many circumstances are difficult to predict, such as the question you will get, ideas you will have, what your mood will be, and who will be in the audience.

The best impromptu speakers know that it is impossible to give stellar answers consistently. Once you accept this fact you not only will stop worrying that your answer won't be good, but you also will give much better answers on average. Your subconscious mind won't be blocked by your worries and will give you great ideas for a speech.

Get familiar with the setting

If you anticipate that you might speak impromptu, get familiar with the setting. To allow your brain to think only about the answer, eliminate the elements that are unfamiliar to you and that can provoke unnecessary fear.

Get on stage and look at the empty audience seats. Sit in different corners of the room. Shake hands and speak with the audience members. The better the connection you feel with the room and the people, the easier it will be for you to think on your feet and connect with the audience.

Once you go on stage, the room will be familiar to you and the audience members will be your allies. You will speak to the audience just as you would to a group of friends in your kitchen. Without fear of the unfamiliar setting and the audience, your brain will concentrate only on thinking about the answer.

Most people fear impromptu speaking, but experienced impromptu speakers know its nature and how to reduce it.

Humor

When you speak impromptu, humor may be more important than during the prepared speech. Humor creates a relaxed atmosphere in the audience and puts your listeners at ease while listening.

Good humor can make your audience enjoy your speech more. Good humor can make the audience listen attentively and remember everything you say better. Good humor can make you win an impromptu speaking competition. To use humor effectively, you need to understand what makes people laugh and how to make your speech funnier.

The structure of the joke

Any joke consists of two parts: a setup and a punch line. A setup is the background information that the audience needs to know for a humorous line to be funny.

The punch line is a humorous line that makes the audience laugh. The setup is where the pattern is established and everything goes in the same direction. The punch line is where a train of thought is derailed from a pattern and people laugh. We laugh when our mind is tricked successfully.

For example, "In the 21st century we have an iPhone, an iPad, but no eye contact." In this case "iPhone" and "iPad" set the pattern and the audience expects something like an "iPod" to be next. "Eye contact" derails the sequence from the pattern and makes the phrase funny.

61

Another example is, "Do you know the most effective way to convey information? Telegraph? No. Telephone? No. Tell a woman!" In this case, "telegraph" and "telephone" set the pattern and "tell a woman" is the punch line.

In order for a punch line to be funny, the setup should be known to the audience. If you told a joke in your circle of friends and they were dying from laughter but it didn't have any effect during the presentation you made at work, it means that the first audience knew a setup but the second one didn't.

Exaggeration and Dialogue

My student George once asked, "Andrii, I want to make people laugh but it's quite difficult for me to come up with humorous lines. How can I be funnier while speaking impromptu?"

I said: "George, it's very easy. There is a magical source of humor that can give your speeches an endless amount of funny moments if you know about it. Dialogue and exaggerations are this magical source."

When you speak impromptu, in the majority of cases, people laugh either when you say a dialogue line of the character in your story, or when you show an exaggerated reaction of another character to this line.

If you just add more dialogue and exaggerated reactions there will be enough humor in your speech. Even if you didn't intend for your dialogue lines or exaggerated reactions to be funny, often people will laugh anyway.

My analysis of thousands of speeches shows that dialogue and exaggerations contain many more funny moments for the audience than other parts of the speech. Use the magic source of humor and you will notice that your audience members laugh much more often than before.

An impromptu speech needs to be succinct

Usually an impromptu speech is only 1-3 minutes long and you need to be succinct in order to convey your message and to make it crisp. Each word that you say either adds or detracts value from your speech and there is no middle ground. Following the recommendations below will significantly reduce the amount of unnecessary words in your speeches.

Avoid filler words

Avoid filler words such as "um," "ah," "basically," "you know," etc. These words just irritate the audience and don't add any value. If you don't know what to say or just feel nervous, instead of using a filler word take a pause to give yourself a couple of seconds to think.

Don't apologize

Never say "Sorry," "I don't know much about this topic" or "Sorry, I just didn't want to say that." When you apologize on stage, you waste your audience's valuable time and it is quite rude. To apologize in our everyday life is a sign of politeness, but you need to forget about the word "sorry" when you speak impromptu. Never apologize for not knowing the subject because if you are not qualified to speak, why should the audience listen to you?

Your impromptu speech shouldn't be perfect. If you stumbled or said something you didn't want to say, just continue speaking.

Condense stories

Telling a story is a very effective way to answer a question, but for an impromptu answer you need to shorten it.

If you have several events in a story, condense them into the most important one. If you have different characters that are necessary to convey a message, condense the number to 2 or 3. Condense the conversation of the characters to only those phrases that are relevant to your point.

By condensing events, conversations and characters, you will be able to answer a question impromptu with a 2-minute story that usually takes 10 minutes to tell and still convey a point.

Be simple

When you speak impromptu, your vocabulary should be at a level that a 12-year-old kid could understand. Public speaking has changed dramatically over the last 50 years. Great speakers of the past such as Winston Churchill or Abraham Lincoln used long sentences, advanced vocabulary and eloquent words, but the greatest speakers of today use much simpler language in their speeches.

A good impromptu speaker needs to be genuine on stage and speak to the audience just as he or she would speak to a friend in everyday conversation. Today people speak in short sentences and use simple language in everyday communication. This is reflected in public speaking, too.

Very often I see speakers who either try to hide their incompetence behind professional terms and abbreviations or try to speak eloquently to look better than they actually are. Unfortunately for them, if the audience notices that a speaker is not genuine, they stop listening to the speech and trusting the speaker.

The greatest experts, leaders and speakers can always explain the most difficult concepts with very simple words and visual examples that even a 12-year-old kid can understand.

If a 12-year-old kid can't understand what you mean, then an engineer with two university degrees won't either. Believe me, an engineer in the past, with two university degrees, who has heard thousands of technical presentations.

If you want to be an effective impromptu speaker and make your speech valuable for the audience, be simple.

Don't strive to be perfect

In impromptu speaking, a perfect speech is a terrible speech. If your speech is very well polished and doesn't have any flaws, your audience will notice that you reproduced the rehearsed text instead of having a genuine conversation with the audience. People like imperfection. They want to see an imperfect, real you.

The expectation for flawlessness in your impromptu speech is much lower than for a prepared speech. Often you will notice that even without a great idea for the answer, without a relevant opening, and with several stumbles, your speech still will be considered great by the audience.

The biggest danger in unprepared speaking lies not in mistakes but in your striving to always give a perfect answer. It blocks quick thinking on your feet, stymies your ability to take risks on stage and lowers your confidence. If you want to become a better impromptu speaker – take risks, forget about being perfect and enjoy your experience on stage.

4 Levels of World-Class Impromptu Speaking

Let's imagine that impromptu speaking is a computer game. This game has 4 levels of difficulty, which you need to go through one by one. After finishing the first 3 levels you will become a really good impromptu speaker, but only after passing the final 4th level will you become one of the best impromptu speakers in the world. Are you ready to play? Let's begin.

Level 1: Speak for 2 minutes

At this level you need to overcome the brain freeze when your mind is going blank and become confident that you can easily speak for 2 minutes on any topic without preparation.

The first level is basic but the most fundamental one. At this level, your only goal is to speak about anything for 2 minutes. Don't worry about whether what you say makes sense. Don't worry about structure or delivery. The only goal is to fill 2 minutes with speaking.

Have you ever seen speakers who stumble and get embarrassed while answering a question impromptu? These speakers still haven't passed through level 1. No matter how experienced you are, if you are working on polishing your level 1, forget about the quality of your speech and just fill the time with words.

Once you are very comfortable on level 1, you will never be afraid to speak off the cuff because you will know that no matter what question is asked you will find the words to answer it somehow. Other levels will ensure that your answer is spectacular but first you need to get rid of the fear that you won't find words once you need them.

You can only eat an elephant piece by piece. The same is true for impromptu speaking. Before you have mastered a previous level, don't try to go to the next one and get confused with too many techniques at once. Only once you are absolutely confident with the first level should you move on to level 2.

Level 2: Add structure and sense

Your listeners can remember information and follow your thoughts only if you speak in a structured way. From a high-level perspective, your speech should have an introduction, body and conclusion. At this level you need to be able to use the frameworks easily for structuring your response. In addition, your speech should support a particular point of view and what you speak about should be clear to the audience. While working on this level, don't pay attention to the body language, vocal variety or eye contact. You will have an opportunity to work on all of these on level 3.

Level 3: Delivery

Most of the delivery techniques used in long speeches are applicable for an impromptu speech. On level 3 you should work on gestures, pauses, eye contact, vocal variety and other delivery techniques. The aim of this level is to develop the ability to deliver an impromptu speech with power, passion and charisma. After you finish working on level 3 all your impromptu answers will be perceived well by the audience.

Level 4: Slant

If you feel comfortable with the first three levels, you are already an advanced impromptu speaker. Congratulations! However, to get to the point where your speeches are remembered for years, you need to master level 4.

There are many good impromptu speakers, but very few are great. If you participate in an impromptu speaking competition, all of the contestants are good speakers, but level 4 is what differentiates a winner from the rest. If you see that your impromptu answer is remembered for years after you gave it, then your speech was at level 4.

If your answer is obvious and doesn't have a unique perspective on the question, it's boring and the speech will be quickly forgotten. Your audience can't concentrate on anything that is boring. You need to avoid giving predictable answers and give your speech a slant (unexpected twist).

For example, suppose you are asked, "Where would you like to spend your next vacation and why?" First, think about the most obvious answers that the majority of people would give, such as "I want to go to Mexico and spend some time at the beach because I am very tired at work and just need to relax," "I want to go skiing in Canada with my family. I enjoy skiing and spending time with family is the best vacation for me" or "I will travel around Europe because I enjoy sightseeing and meeting new people."

In a personal conversation such answers will do fine, but you can't answer like that if you want your impromptu speech to be at level 4. Your audience doesn't care about your vacation but cares about what value they can get from your response. Value is your unique life experience, good laughter or unusual point of view.

Once you have decided for yourself what the most obvious answers could be, take your speech in a completely different direction.

For example, "I would like to spend my entire vacation in the office ..." "I would go to jail for 2 weeks ..." "In my life every day is a vacation because ..." "I'd like to fly to the moon with Ricky Martin for a week ..." or "I would like to be invisible during my vacation so that ..." These beginnings of the answer are unusual and will intrigue your audience to hear more.

It's true that very few speakers are at level 4, but it is not difficult at all to get to this level. When you speak in front of the audience, it's not a private conversation anymore and your goal is not to say what you really think but to give value.

Be creative, avoid predictable directions and your speeches will be remembered for years. People will be looking forward to each of your impromptu speeches. Why? Because they will think, "This speaker is awesome. I am intrigued to hear what he will say this time." When you take a stand that is different from the rest, people will notice you.

Additional tips

The tips in this section are as important as the others in the book, but they don't fall into any of the other sections.

Make it a priority to understand a question

Don't answer a question you don't understand. It is better to ask a second time or even a third time rather than to ramble and give a poor answer.

If you speak impromptu in front of a large audience, once you hear a question rephrase and repeat it. By doing so you let everybody hear the question and acknowledge that you understood it.

Acknowledge the importance of the question

If you give impromptu answers during a Q&A session, occasionally say, "That's a very good question" if you really think so.

At the end of your answer you also can ask, "Does that answer your question?" to make sure that you answered a question sufficiently. These phrases connect you with your audience because they show that you not only listen to people, but also hear them and care that they get good answers.

Time yourself

Make sure that your answers are brief and don't exceed 3 minutes on average. If your answers are long, people will be afraid to ask further questions because they don't want to prolong the presentation significantly if they are seeking to leave on time.

The longer you speak, the more likely you are to lose the attention of the audience. After 2 minutes, it is more and more difficult to keep your audience engaged and excited about the answer.

No matter how much you know about the subject, avoid giving impromptu answers that are longer than 5 minutes. Suggest discussing a topic in more detail either during the break or the next time. Long responses may be irritating and boring for the audience. Impromptu answers are supposed to be short.

Personalize your speech

When you give an impromptu answer, your personal experience and perspective hold more value than facts, statistics or any information that is available on the internet.

Your audience members want to learn your experience, little-known facts and your unique perspective. You, as a speaker, are interested in giving value to the listeners and making their lives better by your answer.

Make your speech as personal as possible to connect with the audience and to make it world class. Refer to the audience, use examples from your personal life and talk about issues that are important to the people who listen to you. Generic, dry answers never achieve anything besides boring the audience. Personal answers are remembered for years and sometimes have the power of changing lives.

Visualize your impromptu speech

A study was done a while back with Olympic runners and visualization. The runners were split into two groups, those who practiced for several hours a day and those who split the same amount of hours between practicing and visualizing themselves running.

The results were astonishing. Those runners who practiced without visualization showed very little improvement in their times, but those who mixed visualization with their training showed great improvement over their previous times.

Michael Jordan visualized not only games, but also winning. This allowed him to win game after game during his extraordinary career. Visualization techniques also work amazingly well in impromptu speaking.

Before coming on stage, visualize yourself giving an outstanding impromptu speech. Clearly imagine the smiles and applause of the audience. Imagine how great it will feel when you succeed. Your thoughts will send the signal to your subconscious and it will make your imagined scene a reality.

It's difficult to describe how the law of positive visualization functions from a scientific point of view, but it works for the greatest athletes, it works for the greatest impromptu speakers, and it will certainly work for you.

Where to find material for impromptu speeches?

Your answer depends not only on your impromptu speaking skills but also on your life experiences. The stories you tell, the examples you provide, and points you make are taken from the life you have lived, and the more versatile it is, the more interesting and valuable your impromptu speeches are.

Remember that people come to hear you primarily because of your unique life experience, not because you have great gestures or vocal variety. It is relatively easy to significantly increase the number of potential stories and experiences in your life that can be used later in impromptu speaking if you develop the right habits.

People tend to stick to routines and spend most days the same way. Because of this, when you are meeting your old friend or a schoolmate and ask, "Hey, haven't seen you in ages. What's happened in the last 5 years?" you may hear a response such as, "Nothing special. I work at the same company. Family is doing fine. We plan to go to Mexico for vacation in the summer." When you change patterns in your life and do what you have never done before, your new experiences result in interesting stories. Here are the habits of world-class impromptu speakers.

Go to places you have never been to before

First of all, travel. Go to other countries, states or cities. Some of the greatest memories of your life may come from travelling. When you change the environment, some of the greatest adventures of your life happen.

Go to an unusual restaurant that you have never been to. If you are not a football fan, go to a football game. If you have never been to a salsa dance party, visit one. If you have never had an interest in art – go to an art gallery.

After such experiences, you might not become a fan of football, salsa or art, but going to a place you have never been before will give you great new ideas that are invaluable not only for impromptu speaking but also for having an interesting and versatile life.

Try new experiences

Try new experiences and activities at least once in your life. If you have never played golf, driven a motorcycle or danced tango, try it once. You shouldn't become an expert in all the activities, but having tried those things at least once will give you great material for future impromptu speeches. Moreover, your perspective on the activity as a person who is trying it for the first time certainly will be fresh, interesting and sometimes hilarious.

Meet new people

In modern society, we tend to limit our communication to only those people we already know. However, a new person can open a new world for you. New acquaintances can bring great new opportunities or ideas into your life, which may be invaluable material for your future impromptu speeches.

When you fly in an airplane, try to start a conversation with the person sitting next to you. Talk to people in a bar, a museum or an art gallery. You never know what this new connection can lead to and what you can learn from any particular person.

Once I had a conversation with a man who is a co-owner of a big boxing magazine and was a professional boxer in the past. I learned so much about boxing and publishing that day. On another occasion, I talked with a guy in a bar whose hobby is fire swallowing. Had I not started the conversation with these people I would never know much about boxing or fire swallowing.

Read books

Books are the quickest and cheapest way to get an education in any area. I think books are very much underestimated in society in terms of the value they can give a reader. You can read a distilled experience that the author gathered for decades within several hours. The core idea here is to read books about areas you know nothing about. Most important for impromptu speaking is not the depth of your knowledge but its versatility.

Having developed the habit of doing what you have never done before will bring you such an amazing pool of interesting ideas and experiences that you will never struggle with finding something interesting to talk about in your impromptu speech. You need to live an interesting life to be an interesting impromptu speaker and an interesting person to talk to.

Stages of learning

Psychologists have researched how adults learn and figured out that adults learn new skills by going through the same 4-stage process. Impromptu speaking is not an exception. In order to truly become a world-class impromptu speaker, you need to go through the entire process.

Unconscious incompetence

Unconscious incompetence is a stage at which you just don't know what you don't know. I may ask you, "Is it easy for you to speak impromptu?" Your response may be totally confused because you never spoke impromptu before and you don't know whether it is difficult.

You may say, "Oh, it is not that difficult because I speak easily without preparation with my friend and I think speaking in front of an audience is pretty much the same."

Conscious incompetence

After you give your first impromptu speech you may think, "Oh, it's much more difficult than I thought. My mind went blank when I needed it the most, I didn't come up with any reasonable answer, I stumbled and felt miserable on stage."

This is a stage of conscious incompetence where you realize what you don't know. Only at the stage of conscious incompetence can you look for resources to learn a new skill. For example, you may decide to sign up for a training, buy a book or ask a more experienced friend for advice.

Conscious competence

After reading this book, you will be at the level of conscious competence. You consciously know all the techniques that will make you an effective impromptu speaker. Once you go on stage and implement new strategies for speaking off the cuff, you see initial results but also experience failures. You may struggle to remember all the techniques and occasionally you may implement them awkwardly.

The level of conscious competence is very dangerous. If you leave your skill at this level, with time you will forget all the knowledge you acquired and may stay at the same level you were before reading the book or trying new techniques. To truly master impromptu speaking or any other skill, you need to get it to the level of unconscious competence.

Unconscious competence

After you have thoroughly practiced the new impromptu speaking techniques that you learned in the book, they will become part of you. You will not need to remember anything you read because you will know it on a subconscious level. Speaking impromptu will be as natural for you as brushing your teeth or walking.

Imagine that you see in the eyes of your audience members that they enjoy your speech but you didn't put much effort into it. How does it sound? Few things can be more fun than speaking impromptu in front of a large audience.

I want you to become an outstanding impromptu speaker who can change lives and whose speeches are remembered for years. However, for my wish to come true you need to raise your impromptu speaking skill to the level of unconscious competence and for this you need to practice.

Where to practice?

If you want to become a great impromptu speaker, knowing the greatest techniques is not enough. You need practice to internalize them. You may ask, "Andrii, where can I safely practice speaking impromptu?" Actually, there are several great options.

Toastmasters clubs

Toastmasters International is an educational organization that runs more than 128,000 clubs worldwide intended to develop public speaking skills of its members. A typical session of the Toastmasters club involves giving prepared speeches, an evaluation section and a table topics session.

During the table topics session members of the club give impromptu speeches that last for 1-3 minutes. Toastmasters club is a unique place where you can practice new impromptu speaking techniques in a safe environment. No matter how you screw up on stage, you will hear applause and words of encouragement.

I highly recommend that you read more about Toastmasters at www.toastmasters.org, find a nearby club and visit it as a guest to decide if you want to become a member later. Once you are a member, volunteer to speak impromptu as often as possible.

With partners

Find a partner and practice together answering different questions impromptu. It really may be a very interesting way to spend time together and have fun. Try doing various exercises from this book in a pair or a group. Let your partner give you feedback about what you did great and how you could have improved your answer.

Practice alone

Practice impromptu speaking exercises on your own. They will greatly prepare you for actual impromptu speeches. When you are in a car, when you are walking or sitting in an armchair, pick an exercise or a question and try to speak for 2 minutes.

To grow very fast in impromptu speaking you need more practice. Practicing alone might not be as effective as in a group, but you can practice alone as much as you want and it is still effective.

After having answered several dozens of questions impromptu, you will notice that you are entering into the high-performance state faster, that topics repeat themselves, and that your answers get better and better because you have mastered the fundamental techniques.

Train your brain to answer impromptu questions as often as possible and you will notice that you are looking forward to the next opportunity to speak off the cuff because you are good at it and it is fun.

Final Checklist

Five minutes before you have to speak impromptu, it's difficult to go through the entire book or remember all the articles you have ever read to make sure you implement the best techniques. However, it is possible to go through a short checklist. Below you can find my checklist that I go through before going on stage.

1. Use the rule of the first thought.

2. Add an unusual slant to the answer.

3. Be genuine.

4. Be energetic.

5. Tell details.

6. My audience members are the best people in my life and my goal is to change their lives for the better.

7. Impromptu speaking is a game. I will have fun on stage.

Most speakers come on stage without keeping anything in mind and hope for luck. Seven is a lucky number and I am sure if you keep this checklist in mind you will be lucky on stage every time you speak and your speech will be outstanding.

Let's put everything together

Imagine that you won $1M in a lottery. How would you spend it?

One night, two years ago, I had a vivid dream. I was sitting in a huge boardroom at an oak table. If you were standing behind me, you could see Warren Buffett sitting across the table and looking right into my eyes.

"Andrii, imagine that Bill Gates gave you one million dollars. What would you spend it on?"

"I would travel around the world for 6 months on a luxurious yacht."

"Andrii, why didn't you make this trip yet?"

"Well, Warren, I don't have $200,000 to buy a yacht."

"Andrii, you don't need to buy a yacht for the trip, you can rent it. I think renting it for 6 months will cost about $20,000. I have never heard of anyone going on such an adventure alone. Find 10 like-minded people who share your dream and split the costs with them.

You see, you need only $2,000 now to fulfill your dream instead of $200,000. If you clean toilets for several months, you can save enough money to make your dream a reality.

If you really wanted to go on this trip you would have found opportunities to do so. I don't believe that you want to travel around the world badly enough."

At that moment I woke up. I couldn't forget about the dream for several months. I thought, "Warren was right. I don't want a trip around the world on a yacht. Everything I wanted badly enough in my life I already have."

I'd like to say, "Bill Gates, once I have a burning desire for something I will find the money and opportunities myself. Give a million dollars to somebody who needs it more than I do. What I really need is more worthy dreams that I want badly enough."

Now read the speech again but with comments about how the principles described in the book are applied in this short impromptu speech. It's not only important to know the techniques but also to see how they are applied.

Imagine that you won $1M in a lottery. How would you spend it? (With comments)

One night, two years ago, I had a vivid dream. I was sitting in a huge boardroom at an oak table. If you were standing behind me you could see Warren Buffett sitting across the table and looking right into my eyes. *(The details make a scene more vivid in the imagination of the audience.)*

"Andrii, imagine that Bill Gates gave you one million dollars. What would you spend it on?" *(I slightly alter a question to one I really want to answer. Instead of answering a question about how I will spend one million dollars won in a lottery, I am answering a question about how I will spend money given by Bill Gates.)*

"I will travel around the world for 6 months on a luxurious yacht." *(Dialogue makes the speech real for the listener as the action in a story unfolds in real time. You can not only learn about what Warren told me but also experience it yourself.)*

"Andrii, why didn't you make this trip yet?"

"Well, Warren, I don't have $200,000 to buy a yacht."

"Andrii, you don't need to buy a yacht for the trip, you can rent it. I think renting it for 6 months will cost about $20,000. I have never heard of anyone going on such an adventure alone. Find 10 like-minded people who share your dream and split the costs with them.

You see, you need only $2,000 now to fulfill your dream instead of $200,000. If you clean toilets for several months, you can save enough money to make your dream a reality.

If you really wanted to go on this trip you would have found opportunities to do so. I don't believe that you want to travel around the world badly enough."

At that moment I woke up. I couldn't forget about the dream for several months. *(I decided to present my story in the form of a dream. In a dream you can make your imagination go wild and nobody in the audience will wonder how you met Warren Buffett in person, flew to Mars or led a platoon of ninja turtles into battle.)*

I thought, "Warren was right. I just don't want a trip around the world on a yacht. Everything I wanted badly enough I already have." *(Here my thoughts are presented in the form of a dialogue.)*

I'd like to say, "Bill Gates, once I have a burning desire for something I will find the money and opportunities myself. Give a million dollars to somebody who needs it more than I do. What I really need is more worthy dreams that I want badly enough."

(Here the conclusion ties to the beginning of the speech, which makes it circular. I take a stand and make clear what I will do in case Bill Gates offers me $1M. You can also see an unusual twist in the speech.

Most people would say, "I would buy a Ferrari or I would donate money to charity," but I took an unusual direction and said that I would refuse the money. Remember, a slant is required to make a speech memorable.)

As you can see the speech has a structure: opening, body and conclusion which makes it easier for the audience to follow and remember. The question was answered with a story, which evokes pictures in the imagination.

Also, as you can see, the vocabulary used in the speech is at a level that a 12-year-old kid can understand. As this impromptu answer is only 2 minutes long the story is succinct. Right from the beginning it gets to the core action and the point of the speech.

When you listen to the answers of other speakers at Toastmasters, on Youtube or at a corporate meeting, try to evaluate them silently based on the principles described in the *Magic of Impromptu Speaking* system. By evaluating others, you will learn the principles faster yourself.

Don't stop until...

I don't know how it happened but in 7th grade I passed the entrance exams into one of the best schools for math in the Ukraine. Six months later my mom was standing in the office of my algebra and geometry teacher, Alexander.

"Victoria, your son's performance is very poor. Honestly, I think math isn't his thing. It would be better for Andrii if you transfer him to another school at the end of the year."

In the afternoon I saw my mom crying, "Andrii,I graduated from school with distinction, your grandma graduated from school with distinction. Why are you studying so badly? I have been explaining basic math to you for hours, but you don't remember a thing. You could end up becoming a street cleaner."

When I was 12 years old, I didn't care about my grades. I didn't care about getting a higher education and I didn't care about my future. I knew only one thing, "If I don't like doing something, I'll avoid it by all means and studying at school is one of those things." I would probably have become a street cleaner if not for one event.

One day Alexander gave us an algebra problem for homework. I obviously couldn't solve it and went to my mom for help. After about 10 minutes, she explained the solution to me.

During the next lesson, Alexander told the class, "Please raise your hand if you have solved the problem I gave you last time." No one besides me raised their hand. "All right, Andrii, please solve the problem on the blackboard."

After I explained the solution Alexander said, "Andrii, Andrii … You solved the problem that even the best students in the class couldn't. I respect you for this. You are cool."

I didn't solve the problem myself, but I enjoyed the feeling of being in front of the class and getting recognition from Alexander. Never before had I felt so good.

Starting that day, there weren't any problems I couldn't solve. Alexander called me to the blackboard only for the problems that nobody else solved. I was looking forward to the toughest problems because I knew that I would be called to the blackboard and would experience my minute of fame again.

I didn't do well in other subjects, but now math became my thing. It actually became my life. I did math at home, I did math during literature classes, and I did math while sleeping. Sometimes I woke up to write down the solution to a problem that came to me in a dream.

One day when we were studying the arithmetic progressions, Alexander gave us a problem, "Please calculate the sum of the row $(1^2+2^2+3^2+4^2...+n^2)$. By the way, in my career there was no student who solved this problem." Can you imagine what I was thinking?

When I came home, I went to the kitchen, took several sheets of paper from my bag and started working on the problem. My reputation at school was at stake. At 1 a.m. my mom said, "Andrii, it's late. Go to bed. How is it going with that math problem, by the way?"

"Mom, I see why nobody solved it before. It's insanely difficult. I tried everything and now just ran out of ideas."

For the next 4 weeks I was living at that table when I wasn't at school or sleeping. Now I clearly remember that table, I clearly remember the shirt I wore and I clearly remember that the solution I came to eventually took 5 sheets of paper. This problem was clearly one of the biggest challenges in my life.

After I shared my solution with the class, Alexander said, "Andrii, that's really impressive. You solved a problem that no student in my career within the last 25 years solved. I respect you. You are a warrior."

Eugen, the guy who sat behind me, whispered, "Sedya (my nickname at school), why are you so stupid, but so good at solving math problems?"

Alexander asked me, "Andrii, can you share with the class your secret approach for solving problems?"

"It took me 3 full weeks to solve the problem with the sum of the row. When I am working on a difficult problem I take a paper out of my bag and don't finish until it is solved, no matter how long it takes."

In 8th grade I became the best student in my math class. By the end of school I had won numerous math competitions. I graduated from the most prestigious technical college in the country and studied in the same group with winners of international school Olympiads in math and programming.

I am insanely grateful to Alexander for showing what success is early in my life. You know why? Because success can be replicated and the process of achieving it in any area is the same.

I repeated what I learned while learning math in IT while working as an engineer at Cisco Systems. I repeated the same process when applying to one of the best MBA programs in the USA, and I repeated it in karate school and it always worked.

In my life I never relied on talent because I know that I am not particularly talented in anything. When I want something really badly I rely on the process that I came to at the age of 12: "I start working on achieving my dream and don't stop until it comes true and it doesn't matter how long it takes."

I hope that impromptu speaking skills will help you in whatever you do. No matter how long it takes, don't stop working towards your dream until it comes true. Luck smiles on the stubborn ones.

Final thoughts

Obviously, impromptu speaking overlaps with prepared public speaking in many regards. I highly recommend you read *Magic of Public Speaking: A Complete System to Become a World Class Speaker*. By using this system, you can unleash your public speaking potential in a very short period of time.

True mastery comes with practice. Join a nearby Toastmasters club and volunteer as often as possible to speak impromptu. Find like-minded friends and practice different questions and exercises together.

After some time, the techniques you learned in *Magic of Impromptu Speaking* will become part of you. To learn more recent tips and techniques I encourage you to visit my website at www.MagicOfPublicSpeaking.com.

If you enjoyed reading this book as much as I enjoyed writing it, I would appreciate your honest review on Amazon.

One Last Thing ...

There is nothing more pleasant for a teacher than to see his students succeed. Begin implementing the *Magic of Impromptu Speaking* techniques in your next impromptu speech and send me an email with your success story to andrii@magicofpublicspeaking.com. I hope to hear from you soon!

Top 100 table topic questions for practice

After a certain amount of practice, you will notice some patterns in topics and genres of questions. The number of completely different questions you may be asked is limited and by practicing you may exhaust all of them.

In this section you will find 100 interesting questions and statements that you can use for practice in a group of fellow impromptu speakers. Your goal is either to answer a question or to share your opinion about a statement in the form of a short speech.

1. Who was your hero when you were a child?

2. Which historical figure do you find the most interesting?

3. Do you think we should have censorship?

4. Do you support the death sentence?

5. What is your view on gun control?

6. You should always tell the truth because …

7. Is marriage an outdated institution?

8. Females make better bosses.

9. Do prisons serve a useful purpose in our society?

10. Money can buy anything and everything.

11. To me, success in life means …

12. Why are people afraid to fail?

13. What does Christmas mean to you?

14. The best thing about our nation …

15. The worst problem facing our nation today …

16. Are prisons the answer for reducing crime?

17. What can we do to improve the education system?

18. The world seems to be getting smaller because …

19. Is it important to know a second language?

20. Is TV worth watching?

21. Are politics and honesty incompatible?

22. The Olympic Games – how important are they?

23. Is it OK for men to cry?

24. Should the budget for the space program be increased?

25. Should all nuclear weapons be eliminated?

26. What is your biggest regret?

27. The thing I'm most proud of.

28. What makes you happy?

29. What is your favorite travel destination?

30. What is the best movie you have ever seen?

31. What was your favorite subject at school?

32. What is the best meal you ever ate?

33. What has been your most interesting journey?

34. What was your most frightening experience?

35. Who has been the main role model in your life?

36. If I could only accomplish one thing in my life, I would like to …

37. If I were an author, I would write about …

38. If you could be an animal, what would it be?

39. If you had to be a zookeeper for a week, which animals would you prefer to look after?

40. If the world were going to end next week, what would be the last 3 things you do?

41. The best job in the world is...

42. If you didn't need to sleep, how would your life be different?

43. If you had to choose between being smarter or better-looking, which would you choose?

44. Suppose you could go back in time and talk to yourself at the age of 10. What advice would you give yourself?

45. Imagine you have just won the Mr. or Miss Universe pageant, a beauty and talent contest. You need to give a speech on television, expressing how happy you are, saying what the award means to you and thanking everyone.

46. If you were given one million dollars and had to spend it in a month, what would you do?

47. A journey of a thousand miles begins with a single step.

48. If you consult enough experts, it is possible to confirm any opinion.

49. The journey is more important than the destination.

50. A smooth path might get you there faster, but a rough trail teaches you more.

51. If a penguin entered the room, what would you say?

52. Do you think professional athletes are overpaid?

53. If you could do something dangerous just once, without any risk, what would you do?

54. If you could change one thing about the world, what would it be?

55. If you had 6 months with no obligations or financial constraints, what would you do with the time?

56. Is it more fun to be a parent or a child?

57. Who did you want to become when you were a child?

58. Who has been an inspiration to you?

59. Wealth is a means to happiness.

60. Courage is …

61. Where would you choose to live if you had to leave this country?

62. What is your most prized possession?

63. If you had to choose one word to describe yourself, which would you choose and why?

64. Describe a time when you felt really happy about yourself.

65. What excites you?

66. What is the best book you ever read?

67. What is your favorite sport?

68. My most memorable holiday is …

69. Which country would you most like to visit?

70. What do you do for fun and why?

71. I plan to retire early so that I can …

72. The world seems to be getting smaller because …

73. If you could turn back time, what age would you want to be, and why?

74. If I could be president for a day, I'd …

75. Knowledge is power.

76. When you cease to dream you cease to live.

77. Things that are easy are seldom worthwhile.

78. Why do you think Mona Lisa was smiling?

79. Where does the road less traveled lead?

80. You're 15 years old. Convince your parents to let you get a tattoo.

81. Home is where the heart is.

82. The best things in life are free.

83. You can if you think you can.

84. Time and tide wait for no man.

85. Less is more.

86. Imagine the world as a single country. Would it be good for humankind?

87. Which difficulty in life made you stronger?

88. What is the key to happiness?

89. If you were selected to go to the moon with a companion of your choice, who would you choose?

90. If you could be invisible for a day, what would you do?

91. You live next to a nuclear power plant. Defend the place as a nice place to live.

92. Success is a process, not a destination.

93. Your worth consists of what you are and not what you have.

94. The person who says that something can't be done should never interrupt the person who is doing it.

95. If you could meet any celebrity, who would it be?

96. If you could witness one event in history, which would it be?

97. If I were the opposite gender, I'd ...

98. Are demonstrations a waste of time?

99. What is the best or worst present you ever received?

100. What was your favorite subject in school?

If there were a program for impromptu speaking at the university, I would give a degree in it only after you answered all 100 questions in this book. The questions are the most interesting, unusual and versatile that I could find. Once you have answered them using the techniques learned in this book, you can truly award yourself a Masters in Impromptu Speaking and this skill will stay with you forever.

Biography

Andrii Sedniev, MBA, is the founder and trainer of the Magic of Public Speaking system which has helped hundreds of speakers worldwide to unleash their potential in public speaking in a very short period of time. Andrii's students say that the Magic of Public Speaking system is the most complete and powerful public speaking training that they have ever experienced.

At the age of 19, Andrii obtained his CCIE (Certified Cisco Internetwork Expert) certification, the most respected certification in the IT world and became the youngest person in Europe to hold it.

At the age of 23, he joined an MBA program at one of the top 10 MBA schools in the USA. Being the youngest student on the program and at the age of 25 he joined Cisco Systems' Head Office as a Product Manager responsible for managing a router which brought in $1 billion dollars in revenue every year.

These experiences have taught Andrii that success in any endeavor doesn't as much depend on the amount of experience but rather on the processes that you are using. Having dedicated over 10 years to researching and practicing a variety of different techniques, Andrii has created the Magic of Public Speaking system. This system is a comprehensive step-by-step program that will enable you to achieve in 2 months what most speakers never achieve in 10 years.

Magic of Public Speaking

A Complete System to Become a World Class Speaker

The Magic of Public Speaking is a comprehensive step-by-step system for creating highly effective speeches. It is based on research from the top 1000 speakers in the modern world. The techniques you will learn have been tested on hundreds of professional speakers and work! You will receive the exact steps needed to create a speech that will keep your audience on the edge of their seats. The book is easy to follow, entertaining to read and uses many examples from real speeches. This system will make sure that every time you go on stage your speech is an outstanding one.

Made in the USA
San Bernardino, CA
15 January 2015